All-Star Players™

MEET PEYTON MANNING

Football's Top Quarterback

John Smithwick

PowerKiDS press

New York

Published in 2007 by The Rosen Publishing Group, Inc.
29 East 21st Street, New York, NY 10010

First Edition

Editor: Jennifer Way
Book Design: Greg Tucker
Photo Researcher: Sam Cha

Photo Credits: Cover, pp. 1, 4, 14 (inset), 21, 22, 29 © Andy Lyons/Getty Images; p. 6 © Otto Greule Jr./Getty Images; p. 8 © Chris Trotman/Getty Images; pp. 10, 16 © Jamie Squire/Allsport; p. 12 © Streeter Lecka/Getty Images; pp. 13 (top), 28 © Doug Pensinger/Getty Images; p. 13 (bottom) © Harry How/Allsport; p. 14 (main) © Jed Jacobsohn/Allsport; p. 17 © Ezra O. Shaw/Allsport; pp. 18, 30 © Peter J. Taylor/Getty Images; pp. 20, 24 © Elsa/Getty Images; p. 26 © Robert Laberge/Getty Images; p. 27 © Rhona Wise/AFP/Getty Images.

Library of Congress Cataloging-in-Publication Data

Smithwick, John.
   Meet Peyton Manning : football's top quarterback / John Smithwick. — 1st ed.
      p. cm. — (All-star players)
   Includes index.
   ISBN-13: 978-1-4042-3634-9 (library binding)
   ISBN-10: 1-4042-3634-1 (library binding)
   1. Manning, Peyton. 2. Football players—United States—Biography—Juvenile literature. I. Title.
   GV939.M289S64 2007
   796.332092—dc22
   [B]
                                    2006019580

Manufactured in the United States of America

Contents

One of Peyton Manning's duties as a quarterback is to tell the rest of his team which plays to make.

Meet Peyton Manning. You may have seen him on TV. He is one of the greatest quarterbacks ever to play the game of football.

The quarterback is the leader of his team's **offense**. He tells the other players on his team how to line up on the field and where to run. During most offensive plays, the quarterback must decide what to do with the football. He can hand it off to a runner. He can throw it down the field to a receiver. He can even run with the ball himself. The quarterback must be able to guess the opposing team's **strategy** and make split-second decisions. A good quarterback must be **athletic** and smart. Peyton Manning is more than just a good quarterback. He is one of the best players in the NFL.

All-Star Stats

Peyton Manning grew up in New Orleans, Louisiana.

5

Passing is another important quarterback skill.

A Football Family

Football has always been an important part of Peyton Manning's life. Quarterback talent runs in his family. Peyton's father, Archie Manning, was a **legendary** quarterback at the University of Mississippi. This school is also called Ole Miss. Today, the speed limit on the Ole Miss streets is 18 miles per hour (29 km/h), in honor of Archie Manning's number. After college Archie Manning played in the NFL for the New Orleans Saints, the Houston Oilers, and the Minnesota Vikings. After he stopped playing football, Archie Manning was a color commentator. A color commentator is a person who talks about a sport on the radio or TV.

All-Star Stats

As a kid Manning sometimes joined in the Saints practices and workouts.

Peyton's younger brother Eli (left) plays for the New York Giants. Here are the Manning brothers in 2004.

Peyton's younger brother Eli is also a quarterback. He plays for the New York Giants. The Manning brothers played against each other at the beginning of the 2006 season. This game marked the first time in NFL history that brothers played as quarterbacks against each other.

While growing up Manning got to spend time with his father's teammates. He paid close attention to how they practiced and played football. By the time he was old enough to play the game himself, Manning already knew how to be a good player.

Here is Peyton with his father, Archie Manning (right). Peyton was playing with the Volunteers at this time.

At College

Manning went to college at the University of Tennessee and was the quarterback for his school's football team, the Tennessee **Volunteers**.

After his third year in college, Manning had the chance to leave school and enter the NFL. Many coaches and sports journalists agreed that he was ready to play on the **professional** level. Manning believed that school was just as important as professional football. He decided to stay in college for a fourth year so he could play one more season with the Volunteers. He graduated with honors. In fact Manning had the highest grade point average of anyone in his field of study.

While playing for the Volunteers, Manning threw for 11,201 yards and set 42 passing records. The University of Tennessee honored Manning by retiring his number, 16. This means that no other Volunteers player will ever wear the number 16

Manning is holding a framed shirt that bears his retired Volunteers number.

again. It belongs to Manning forever. In over 60 years, the school has retired the numbers of only 12 other players.

Manning's college football career captured the attention of the entire sports-watching world. Now that he had won many **accolades** in college, he was ready for the NFL. Which lucky team would he play for?

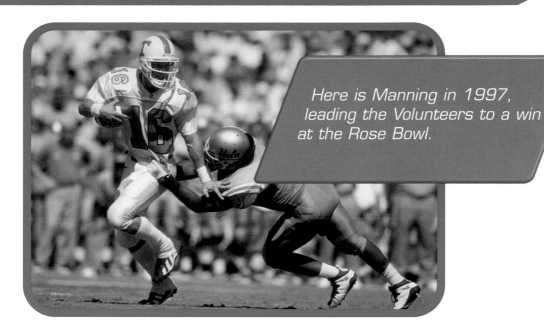

Here is Manning in 1997, leading the Volunteers to a win at the Rose Bowl.

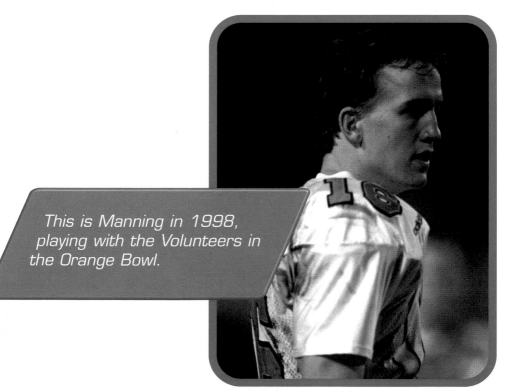

This is Manning in 1998, playing with the Volunteers in the Orange Bowl.

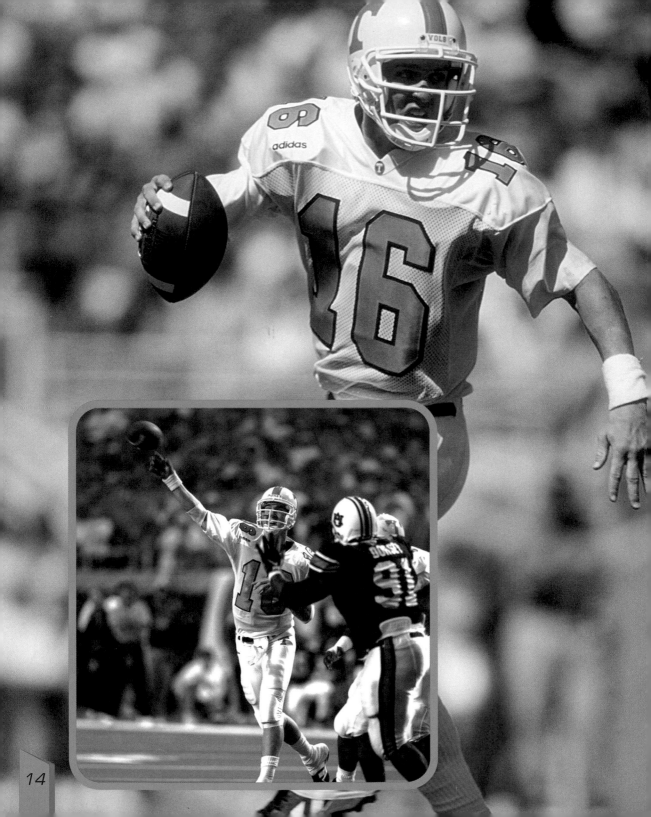

The NFL Draft

In April of 1998, Peyton Manning entered the NFL draft. During the draft the NFL teams choose the best college athletes to play for them. There are seven rounds in the draft. Each NFL team gets to pick one player each round.

The draft was started to help bad teams get better. The worst teams get to choose players before the best teams. The team that had the worst record of the last season gets to choose first. The team that won the Super Bowl must choose last. This method makes sure that the best college players go to teams that really need their talent. Manning was sure to be a top pick in the draft. Not only was he one of the best athletes, but he was seen as ready to handle the **pressure** of playing in the NFL.

Peyton Manning's excellent record playing for the Volunteers (opposite and inset) made him a top NFL draft pick.

Peyton and his father, Archie, appeared together at Madison Square Garden in New York City during the 1998 NFL Draft.

In 1997, the Indianapolis Colts finished in last place in their division, or grouping. This meant they had the first choice in the 1998 NFL Draft. There were 241 players drafted that year, and the

Colts chose Manning first. The Colts would soon find out that they made a good choice.

Here is Manning soon after he was chosen by the Indianapolis Colts.

The other top pick in the 1998 draft was Ryan Leaf. He no longer plays in the NFL and is considered one of football's biggest letdowns.

In his first season with the Colts, Manning posed for an official picture.

Playing for the Colts

Peyton Manning had been such a good college player that expectations for his professional playing were very high. His teammates, his coaches, and his new fans were depending on him to play well. The sports **media** were also watching him closely. If he did not play well, the media would say bad things about him on TV, in the newspapers, and on the radio. That is a lot of pressure. This might be the reason that Manning loves the following saying about pressure. Chuck Knoll, a past coach of the Pittsburgh Steelers, said that "pressure is something you feel only when you don't know what you're doing." It is clear that Manning knows what he is doing.

Manning won the Most Valuable Player **award**, or MVP, in both 2003 and 2004. This means he did more to help his team's success than any

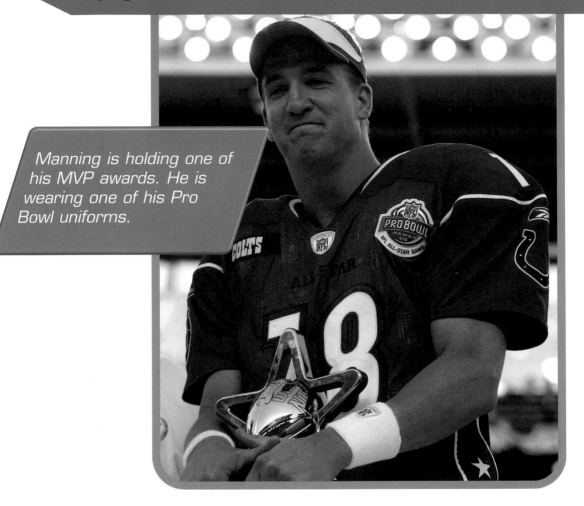

Manning is holding one of his MVP awards. He is wearing one of his Pro Bowl uniforms.

other player in the NFL. He is only the third player in history to win the MVP award in back-to-back seasons.

Manning has been chosen to appear in five Pro Bowls. The Pro Bowl is a football game played by only the very best players from each team. He is

Manning is being sacked, or tackled, during a game against the New England Patriots.

the first quarterback ever to make more than 4,000 passing yards in six straight seasons. He is also the first quarterback to throw 25 or more touchdown passes in seven straight seasons. Thanks to Manning the Colts are now a huge force in the NFL.

When he is not on the field, Manning actively runs the PeyBack Foundation's charities.

The PeyBack Foundation

Football is not Peyton Manning's only job. He also runs his own **charity**. Manning started the PeyBack Foundation in 1999. It organizes educational, leadership, and athletic **events** for children from poor families and communities. The PeyBack Foundation has donated nearly $1 million to youth charities. Manning serves as president of the foundation, and he oversees all its important decisions.

The Peyback Classic is the foundation's most famous event. At the PeyBack Classic, high-school football teams get to play at the RCA Dome, where the Colts play their home games. These are teams from schools with very little money to spend on athletics. The money from the event goes directly to the schools.

Manning takes time out to meet with fans and sign helmets and footballs.

Another popular PeyBack event is the PeyBack Bowl. At the PeyBack Bowl, Manning throws a bowling party and asks famous people to come to the bowling lanes to help him raise money for the foundation. Famous Indianans such as singer John Mellencamp, Indianapolis Pacers basketball player Reggie Miller, and the Colts coach Tony Dungy have all played.

The Peyback Foundation also offers **grants** to teachers and schools. It supplies holiday meals for poor children and their families. Manning considers his work with the PeyBack Foundation as important as anything he has accomplished on the football field.

Manning is waving to fans after the game in which he broke Dan Marino's record of 48 touchdowns in one season.

Peyton Plays On

In 2005, it looked like Peyton Manning and the Colts would finish the season undefeated, or without losing a game. No team has accomplished this since the Miami Dolphins in 1972. The Colts won their first 13 games. They had only three games to play to finish undefeated, but they finally lost to the San Diego Chargers. The Colts still had a better record than any other football team.

The 2005 postseason was one of the best for the Indianapolis Colts.

Although they did not make it to Super Bowl XL, Peyton Manning and the Colts had a great 2005–2006 season.

Manning and the Colts entered the 2005 play-offs with the top **seed** in the American Football **Conference**. Most sports journalists expected them to go to the Super Bowl. Unfortunately, the Colts fell short of that goal. They lost to the Pittsburgh Steelers, 21–18, in one of the closest games of the year.

In just seven years with the Colts, Manning has done more than any other quarterback in football history. The only accomplishment he still has yet to do is to win the Super Bowl. Maybe he will do it in the coming years.

Manning hopes to fulfill his dream of winning the Super Bowl one day.

Height: 6'5" (2 m)
Weight: 230 pounds (104 kg)
Team: Indianapolis Colts
Uniform Number: 18
Date of Birth: March 24, 1976
Draft Pick: 1998, first round
Years in NFL: 9

2005–2006 Season Passing Stats

Passes Attempted	Passes Completed	Total Yards	Touchdowns	Interceptions	Quarterback Rating
453	305	3,747	28	10	104.1

Career Passing Stats as of 2005–2006 Season

Passes Attempted	Passes Completed	Total Yards	Touchdowns	Interceptions	Quarterback Rating
4,333	2,769	33,189	244	130	93.5

Glossary

accolades (A-kuh-laydz) Special honors.

athletic (ath-LEH-tik) Having ability and training in sports and exercises of strength.

award (uh-WORD) A special honor given to someone.

charity (CHER-uh-tee) A group that gives help to the needy.

conference (KON-frens) A grouping of sports teams.

events (ih-VENTS) Things that happen.

grants (GRANTS) Money given for a certain purpose.

legendary (LEH-jen-der-ee) Of or relating to a person who has been famous and honored for a very long time.

media (MEE-dee-uh) Journalists and people who appear on TV and radio shows.

offense (AH-fens) When a team tries to score points in a game.

pressure (PREH-shur) The weight of feeling worried about something.

professional (pruh-FESH-nul) Paid to do something.

seed (SEED) A player or team that has been given a position for a group of play-off games, often at a given level.

strategy (STRA-tuh-jee) The planning and directing of movements on the field.

volunteers (vah-lun-TEERZ) Soldiers who had jobs outside the military before the war. Tennessee's nickname is the "Volunteer State."

Index

Web Sites

Due to the changing nature of Internet links, PowerKids Press has developed an online list of Web sites related to the subject of this book. This site is updated regularly. Please use this link to access the list:
www.powerkidslinks.com/asp/peyton/